# THINGS I NEVER SAID TO MYSELF

# THINGS I NEVER SAID TO MYSELF

Duduzile Noeleen Ngwenya

AMARYLLIS

AMARYLLIS

An imprint of Manjul Publishing House Pvt. Ltd.
• C-16, Sector 3, Noida, Uttar Pradesh 201301, India
Website: www.manjulindia.com
*Registered Office:*
• 10, Nishat Colony, Bhopal 462 003 – India
*Distribution Centres*
Ahmedabad, Bengaluru, Bhopal, Chennai, Hyderabad,
Kolkata, Mumbai, Noida, Pune

*Things I Never Said to Myself* by Duduzile Noeleen Ngwenya



This edition first published in India in 2024
Second impression 2024

**ISBN 978-93-5543-653-5**

Printed and bound in India by Thomson Press (India) Ltd.

*To my family,*

*Thank you for always pushing me to be my best self and allowing me to live. If I had to be reborn, I'd choose you to be my family, over and over again.*

**Dear Self,**

**This is a book filled with words I failed to say to you when you needed me to.**

# Contents

# Author's Letter

It's been about three years since I started writing this book. Well, for starters, I'll put it out there that one of the reasons for that is that I felt like it isn't worth being read by the world. That's probably one of the worst ways to convince you to read it until the end, but we're all about allowing ourselves to be human in this space. I'm 26 this year (Aug 2022), and I suddenly got the edge to release this collection because as I went through these notes one night, I realized that everything I wrote was what I needed to hear from myself at different points of my life. So I thought — what if I'm not the only one? I couldn't be more honored now that you're here, reading this, three years later.

I want you to know that you're not the only one in the process of learning how to have a healthy relationship with yourself. We're all trying to figure it out. You start by making an effort in the little things, like how you talk to and about yourself daily. This book is your start. But it will take more than just reading it to get to a point where you're in a good relationship with yourself. Self-love and awareness is a lifetime journey that needs you to be dedicated and very intentional. Be aware of your thought pattern. How does what you think about yourself impact you? Which words or phrases make you feel good about yourself? Which ones make you feel pity, sadness, anxiety, or hopelessness? You've got to know the cause to treat it right.

Many things work differently for everyone, but I hope the words in this Book heal you and give you a fresh start. The good news is that we get countless chances to be good to ourselves. It doesn't matter how long you've had a toxic or dark relationship with yourself. What matters is that you take the step to fix, heal, and restore it.

Thank you for getting your hands on this book. I hope it makes the difference you anticipate and long for. More importantly, I wish you love, warmth and happiness.

Yours,
**Noeleen**

# Collection I

*Growth, love & healing*

(54)

Here's to exploring,
Learning, unlearning,
Living and loving yourself more.

— *noeleensaid*

Breathe.

One day at a time.
One step at a time.
You're doing a lot better than you think.

*– noeleensaid*

Maybe it doesn't get better,
Or perhaps it does.
But ultimately, you get better.
You grow,
You change,
You evolve.

And maybe that's the point.

— *noeleensaid*

Regardless of the painful parts of your past
You still love as if it's the only thing you know.

That's your strength.
I hope you make an effort to embrace your power.

— *noeleensaid*

Being imperfect doesn't make you any less worthy of love,
progression, happiness, or everything beautiful about this world.

– *noeleensaid*

Your experiences are there to show you different
layers of yourself. They're not there to expose your
weaknesses.
Whenever you go through the trials life throws at you,
you learn how to best respond.
When you discover your unpleasant way of dealing with
things,
learn how to soar through those circumstances
with gentleness and warmth.

— *noeleensaid*

Hey,

At this moment, you're in control.
But when it feels like you're not, God is.
Just trust that it's in greater hands.

— *noeleensaid*

What do you do when you feel down?

You breathe,
acknowledge your feelings,
reaffirm,
remind yourself that this is just another phase,
and that it will pass.

— *noeleensaid*

You deserve to be loved unapologetically,
consistently, without asking for it.

Don't be giving out too much.
Don't hold in too much, either.
When it's real, you will know,
Without having to give in more than you should.

— *noeleensaid*

Forgive yourself,

for tolerating the unfairness, other people put you
through,
for not knowing and doing better,
for prioritizing everything and everyone else but
yourself,
for constantly breaking your spirit without realizing it,
for not being kind enough toward yourself.

If you've given so many chances to those who've
wronged you,
what could ever make you less deserving?

— *noeleensaid*

What you constantly feed on; grows.
Whether it's love or hate, it grows.
And it'll reflect through your actions.

Don't feed energies and habits you'll struggle to accommodate.

— *noeleensaid*

We tend to expect from others what we can give,
and this makes us vulnerable.

It's okay to have expectations,
not having any would make you settle for whatever is on the table.
Even so, learn to deal with unmet expectations
without convincing yourself that yours were too high or unrealistic.

– *noeleensaid*

May every phase of your life, in its own way, be gentle to
you.
I hope you'll have a tribe of your own that's constantly
there to help you see your worth.
May you be reminded of the greatness you're destined
for.

— *noeleensaid*

I'm sorry,

That when you felt unappreciated, someone
invalidated you. When you expressed yourself,
you were labelled as "over sensitive".
That you kept meeting people who tried to dim your
light.

Despite it all, do not let them define you.
And remember that no one can dim your light
without your approval. Don't invest yourself in what
cannot make you brighter than you already are.

– *noeleensaid*

When you're hurting,
Allow it for as long as it needs to.
Don't rush your healing.

– *noeleensaid*

Even in the most challenging circumstances,
choose yourself. Don't be one of the people who've
hesitated before they chose you.

— *noeleensaid*

If a relationship feels forced, let it go.
If it doesn't feel mutually beneficial anymore, let it go.
For your sanity, learn to make even the most painful decisions.

It's not worth it to lose yourself for anything or anyone.

– *noeleensaid*

Not everyone you get to love will receive
and reciprocate your love. That doesn't imply that
your love is unacceptable or that you're hard to love.
It simply means you're yet to meet those who deserve it.

– *noeleensaid*

Forgive those who never reciprocate your good
intentions.

May it all be a reminder
to love yourself louder, intentionally,
and enough not to allow yourself to be unappreciated.

— *noeleensaid*

It might not make sense now,
but just like everything else, it will end.
You either learn to live with it or move past it,
but in everything, life gets better, and so do you.

— *noeleensaid*

And on days when you can't show up for yourself?
You breathe.
You let things be.
You allow it.

You remind yourself that there were days when
you showed up for yourself, but today isn't one of them,
and that's okay.

— *noeleensaid*

True happiness involves contentment with
where you are in life. Despite where you want to be or
what you're working toward, treasure even the moments
you'd never choose if you had your way.

Those moments are part of your journey;
they make it what it is. Next time you feel overwhelmed
by the process, remind yourself that those moments
will someday be just a story that adds weight to your
success,
and it will inspire you to continue.

— *noeleensaid*

You're not too sensitive,
You're not weak,
You're not an emotional wreck,
If it hurts you, it hurts you.

Don't invalidate your emotions.

– *noeleensaid*

That unutterable painful past,
uncertainties,
fears,
beautiful memories,
they're all part of your journey.

You cannot select and erase your past,
you can only learn and move past it.
It doesn't define anything in your present,
nor does it equate to your future,
but it is still a part of your life.
Please don't be embarrassed about it.
Don't regret it.
Embrace it.

It makes you who you are.

– *noeleensaid*

Have you looked at yourself lately?
How resilient you've been.
How beautiful you've become.
And just how gracefully you're progressing?

Sometimes your path won't make sense,
but I hope to see you flourish either way.
There are many voices you'll hear along the way;
I hope you only listen to the ones
that remind you how brilliant you are.

— *noeleensaid*

You're going to meet people who won't understand
how delicate you are, people who'll take your way of
expressing disappointment as melodramatic.
In all those moments, may you be able to reaffirm
that you don't have to change anything about who you are.
You're perfect the way you are.

— *noeleensaid*

Blame is a toxic coping mechanism.
We tend to feel better about ourselves
when we don't take responsibility.
Owning up to the part you play in everything is a strength.

*– noeleensaid*

Every time you complain about something;
You miss out on the opportunity to be grateful for
another.

While gratitude brings peace to the heart,
Murmuring takes away a moment of peace you cannot
regain.

— *noeleensaid*

There are more than enough reasons why
you have the insecurities that you have,
but none is big enough to justify why you
cannot make an effort to confront and accept those flaws,
and start working on them.

— *noeleensaid*

Did you try today?
Harder than yesterday?
Try again tomorrow.

And if tomorrow is still the same? Try again the next day.
What's important is that you don't stop trying.
You don't give up.

I long to see you on your brighter days.

— *noeleensaid*

I know it's hard,
I know it hurts,
It's okay to feel like it's too much,
I understand.

Just allow it.
Allow it to hurt,
Allow it not to make sense,
For as long as it takes.

You're going to be okay.
Not today, and maybe not tomorrow,
But eventually, you'll come out stronger,
and things will make sense again.

— *noeleensaid*

I've realized the importance of having something
to look forward to despite how life is going at this
moment.
You need hope, even if it's just a little hope.
Hope for certainty or possibility.
It's what carries you through until you
receive what you're truly longing for.

— *noeleensaid*

At every moment, how you feel is valid.
Don't resist. Acknowledge and reaffirm.
It doesn't matter how it inconveniences anyone,
your feelings are real, and deserve to be acknowledged.

— *noeleensaid*

What if some of the times you thought someone
didn't do enough for you; was because you expected
from them what you could've done for yourself?

— *noeleensaid*

We all need spaces to express ourselves
as genuinely as we can.
To express our sadness, happiness,
hopelessness, hope, dreams,
aspirations, and anxieties.

Such a space can be created within you.
You learn how to allow yourself to be as genuine
as you can with yourself,
without seeing yourself as weak or faulted.

— *noeleensaid*

For different reasons, we are constantly reminded
of our flaws, weaknesses, failures, or what we lack the most.
Consciously choose to dwell on the reasons why
you're so worthy, brilliant and beautiful.
And if you can't find those reasons, look deeper.

— *noeleensaid*

Maybe there are a thousand other people who
can do what you do,
but there's no one else who can do it with your touch,
and that's what makes you one of a kind.

– *noeleensaid*

The energy you choose to surround yourself with
eventually becomes yours. Declutter, set boundaries,
and remove yourself from the lives of people
whose energies don't align with yours.

– *noeleensaid*

While you're learning how to love yourself the way
you need to be loved, the emotions labeled as "negative"
will be harder to deal with.
Don't be hard on yourself on those days.

It's okay to feel angry, sad, anxious, upset,
disappointed, or ashamed. Your emotions don't define you.
They simply mean that you process things your way,
which is valid.

— *noeleensaid*

**Greed**

There's a danger in not being content or satisfied.
Always wanting more, always chasing more,
even when you have enough of something, you never see it,
Because you always want more.
It's not wrong to be ambitious, not to settle for the bare minimum.
But there is a fragile line between ambition and greed.

— *noeleensaid*

Maybe we struggle to accept some things about ourselves
because we've labeled them "negative."
We find it hard to embrace how fragile or sensitive we are,
or how easily we get attached to things/people because we've
taught ourselves that it's a weakness and have to hide it.

You are art.
The sooner you show up as that,
the more you'll understand why it was never necessary for
you to be ashamed of anything you come with.
Remember, everything about art has meaning and purpose.

— *noeleensaid*

You're where you need to be,
at the time you need to be.
Don't ever allow yourself to be under
the pressure of someone else's timeline.

— *noeleensaid*

## A place

Find a place within yourself,
that shares a little kindness when you make mistakes,
that meets you with grace when you're struggling,
that allows you to let yourself be loved.

— *noeleensaid*

This is for all the stolen years.
Where society standards made you believe that
there was an acceptable kind of beauty,
and yours didn't meet that criterion.

When you look in the mirror or take a picture,
see beauty in your uniqueness.
That way, you take back the power that was once
stolen from you.

– *noeleensaid*

My hope for you is that you never let anyone,
and I mean anyone, let you believe that you're not
enough.

— *noeleensaid*

I pray that you get to a point where you only
do things because you want to do them.
Not because someone approves.
When you get to that point,
realize how gratifying it is not to depend on
anyone else's validation but yours.

— *noeleensaid*

Some days,
loving yourself is being able to breathe,
and remind yourself that you're doing okay.

*— noeleensaid*

You've given parts of yourself to people,
some were good, and some weren't.
I hope that you don't spend the rest of your life
withholding yourself because of the people
who didn't appreciate you.

Oh, beloved, you deserve to meet each
and every person who's going to value you.

– *noeleensaid*

Remember the excitement of getting something right,
achieving a goal, making a new friend, starting afresh,
celebrating an anniversary or simply feeling happy.
But also take note of the times you failed to do
something,
got hurt, disappointed, lied to, or felt things weren't
going your way.

Those instances remind us when we need to be
more gentle with ourselves.

— *noeleensaid*

Don't ever associate yourself with small.
In whatever you do or want to do,
don't indulge the thought that you're 'small,'
because your thoughts are so powerful,
that they manifest.

— *noeleensaid*

Know when to give and when to stop giving.
Giving is a kind gesture, but knowing when to stop
is a kinder act toward yourself.

Beloved, those who take don't have limits.

— *noeleensaid*

Meet yourself with a little more grace.
In how long it takes you to heal,
love yourself better, or build something you want.
Most of the time, you're not failing how to do things;
you're just not gracious enough toward yourself.

— *noeleensaid*

You don't need to have it all figured out.
Just give it your best shot,
and let things unfold on their own.

— *noeleensaid*

Comparing yourself to others is normal.
Don't beat yourself up about it.
Gently shift your focus to what makes you who you are,
and why you don't need to be like anyone else.

– *noeleensaid*

# Collection II

*Notes to Self*

(50)

Dear Self,

Please forgive me,
For all the times I unhesitatingly chose other people over you,
For continuously seeking external validation,
For speaking unkindly to you,
For consciously putting you in situations and involving you with people who didn't deserve your presence,
For thinking, you weren't good enough,
And mostly, please forgive me for loving everyone else but you.

I commit myself to do better.
To fill your cup,
And to give you that love I freely to provide others.

Yours truly,
*Myself*

Dear Self,

I applaud you for keeping it together till this very
moment.
I celebrate your resilience.
I've given you little credit for everything you get through,
and I've been unnecessarily hard on you.

But as of now, I consciously choose to find something to
cheer you for.
Here's to your strength and your resilience.

Yours truly,
*Myself*

Dear Self,

Be happy about the gift of life.
If it gets too overwhelming, take a break.
Remind yourself that each day serves a different purpose,
and it's okay to stop just to catch your breath.
However, always continue or start over on another day.

Part of loving yourself better is to know when you need a break.

Yours truly,
*Myself*

Dear Self,

I hope you remember that you are worth it.
You are enough.
You are loved.
You are beautiful.

Affirm yourself every day.
Don't wait for anyone to remind you
of things you ought to know on your own.
Realize and rectify your mistakes.

And remember that the only way to be kind to
others is if you are kinder to yourself.

Yours truly,
*Myself*

Dear Self,

Get up every morning, embracing that
you have the power to set a high tone for your day.
May every day be an opportunity for you to put that
power into practice.

Yours truly,
*Myself*

Dear Self,

I am sorry,

for all the times you felt broken, hopeless,
less worthy or beautiful, sad, played, confused, or
anxious;
for not pushing myself enough to understand that
it was okay for you to feel the way you did;
for not pushing myself enough to know it was okay
for you to need reassurance;
for criticizing your flaws without appreciating your
perfections.

Yours truly,
*Myself*

Dear Self,

**"If it costs your peace, then you can't afford it."**

You have the power to choose how you react.
In as much as some situations or people make it hard to see this,
remember that you have the power.
Do whatever it takes to protect your peace.

Yours truly,
*Myself*

Dear Self,

Breathe.

Allow things to happen at their pace.
Remind yourself that everything that's meant to be will be.
Don't be controlled by fear.
Let go of what doesn't serve you anymore.
Don't be afraid of rejection.
Never hesitate to start.
Take a leap of faith.
Trust yourself through God.

May this day be filled with love, warmth, opportunities,
and fruitfulness.

Yours truly,
*Myself*

Dear Self,

This is a commitment I am making to you,
to stop practicing self-sabotage,
because there's more to you than that.
I commit to doing better for you,
and I will not indulge in what isn't contributing to your growth.

Throughout this journey, may you be
self-resilient, kind, strong, and confident.
May you also allow yourself to be sensitive,
helpless, confused, and anxious.

Yours truly,
*Myself*

Dear Self,

May you grow into the person you envision yourself to be every day.

Yours truly,
*Myself*

Dear Self,

The past is for you to learn,
the present is for you to dwell in,
the future is for you to anticipate and plan for.

You owe it to yourself to make it work today.

Yours truly,
*Myself*

Dear Self,

You're enough,
with or without that person you
think you cannot do without.
Get to a point where you still feel complete
without those you've built homes for in your heart.

You're enough,
Before they came,
While they were here,
And when they left.

Your worth isn't attached to anyone you get to love and care about.

Yours truly,
*Myself*

Dear Self,

Envision the life you want;
believe that you deserve it;
then work on it religiously.

Redirect your energy towards
what you want your life to look like daily.

Yours truly,
*Myself*

Dear Self,

Let your daily prayer be,

"Grant me, oh God, a grateful heart.
May I wake up every morning
appreciating the blessings, you've given me.
Please teach me how to be present in my present.
Please give me the strength to move past what hurts me.
Heal, even the parts of me I did not know were bleeding.
Please help me be productive in all I do.
And teach me how to love those around me, and most importantly myself."

Yours truly,
*Myself*

Dear Self,

*"If you continue to live in the past or the future,*
*you miss out on living in the present.*
*And that's a gift you can never buy or regain."*

Take things as they come.
What happened in the past cannot be altered.
And the future can only be determined
by what you do in the present.

You're capable.

Yours truly,
*Myself*

Dear Self,

You've got to see yourself as what you want to become.

Take a step towards what you want to achieve.
Don't look for reasons why you can't get it.
Dedicate yourself to everything you want,
If it doesn't work out, you lose nothing.
We all deserve what we're working on.

*"I never knew a man that was good at making excuses who was good at anything else."*

Yours truly,
*Myself*

Dear Self,

Your life is going at a pace it's supposed to go.
You're not late or early for anything.
Your progress isn't slow or fast.
There is no universal timeframe for life's progress and success.
Everyone has their own.

You will get to where you are going,
as long as you don't project other people's lives onto yours.

Yours truly,
*Myself*

Dear Self,

Here's to you.

All the battles you've overcome and
the ones you continue to fight daily;
your achievements, whether small or big;
and here's to the failures that turned out to be necessary
lessons.

Here's to exploring possibilities, learning,
unlearning unhealthy habits, living, and loving yourself
more.

Yours truly,
*Myself*

Dear Self,

Thank you for not giving up.
The end of this day, week, month,
or year won't be the end of life,
It will just be another starting point.

Now is your time to finish what you started,
to start what you've contemplated doing.
You have tons of abilities waiting for you to explore.

You can do anything you believe you're capable of doing,
it can never be more or less than that.

Yours truly,
*Myself*

Dear Self,

Have you forgiven me?

For not showing up for you when you needed me the most;
For being hard on you when all you needed was affirmations;
For listening to what people said more than I listened to you;
For being impatient with your progress;
For subconsciously talking you down countless times;
For going back and forth with people who did not deserve to know your soul;
For overlooking the number of times, you came out at the top when you were at your lowest.

Have you forgiven me?
Sometimes the only person you need to forgive is yourself.

Yours truly,
*Myself*

Dear Self,

You've shrunk yourself to fit into spaces you were meant to outgrow,
you've lived to please other people more than yourself,
you've invalidated how you felt,
now is the time you experience the person you were meant to be.

The bold you.
The brave you.
The brilliant you.
The self-loving you.
The version of you that's unapologetic about who you are.

Yours truly,
*Myself*

Dear Self,

Some days are beautiful, refreshing, and calm;
while some are sad and long.
Life is about finding a balance between the two.
Remember that what impacts you the most isn't what
    you go through,
but how you choose to go through it.

Take each day as it comes,
be happy as much as you can,
allow yourself the chance to live
every day as best and genuine as you can.

Yours truly,
*Myself*

Dear Self,

You are capable of growing
in every aspect of your life.
You learn and unlearn,
and you survive.

Through it all,
I hope you find it within yourself
to love, forgive, and keep evolving.

Yours truly,
*Myself*

Dear Self,

The same way you plan for your future,
reflect on how far you've come,
how you've kept it together,
and how you continue to thrive.

In everything, I wish you love, happiness, and strength.
Oh, I'm so proud that you overcame.

Yours truly,
*Myself*

Dear Self,

It's important for you to be happy.
Surround yourself with things and people that cultivate
that feeling.
Be happy about the little things,
how you ticked a task off your to-do list,
how you didn't snooze your alarm,
how you made it through a rough day,
or how you put a smile on someone's face.
I hope you constantly find reasons to be happy.

Yours truly,
*Myself*

Dear Self,

Does it ever click to you that you're doing your best?
That the decisions you made, regardless of how they
turned out,
were the best decisions you could have made at that
moment?

You're doing the best you can.
Despite how things turn out in the end,
you always do what you think is best,
and that is enough.

Yours truly,
*Myself*

Dear Self,

You don't have to keep it together all the time,
you're allowed to break down,
you don't owe strength to anyone.

You owe it to yourself to be as authentic as you can be.

Yours truly,
*Myself*

Dear Self,

I've seen you get better.
I've seen you being extraordinary and confident.
I've seen you being ambitious.

Take every opportunity to meet yourself at your fullest potential.
Go for everything you want, without hesitation.
I am rooting for you.

Yours truly,
*Myself*

Dear Self,

In your quietness, dream and live as great as you can.
In your softness, stand up for yourself.
In your beauty, see the beauty in everything else.
In your ability to love, remember to love yourself more each day.

Yours truly,
*Myself*

Dear Self,

There are days when you can't show up for yourself.
In those days,
don't talk yourself down,
don't force yourself to feel what you're unable to.

Breathe,
Honor your emotions,
Allow yourself to be anything else but strong.

Yours truly,
*Myself*

Dear Self,

Don't hold onto what hurts.
Don't hold onto what makes you feel any less worthy.
There's a side to life that's less painful and more beautiful
than what you might have experienced,
Look for it, and find it.
That's a side you also deserve to live in.

Yours truly,
*Myself*

Dear Self,

I hope you know that…
you're able to achieve whatsoever you put your mind to,
you excel in everything you do,
you feel that you're enough,
and deserving.

Yours truly,
*Myself*

Dear Self,

Take a moment,
Look into what happened during the past week.
How different would you like this week to be?
What changes do you want to see?

Take control.

Until you shift your focus from what you don't want your life to be like, to how you'd ideally like your life to be,
You're not prepared for change.

Yours truly,
*Myself*

Dear Self,

Create a space within yourself
where you can make mistakes, learn, rise,
cry, grow, feel hopeless and have faith again.
A space where you can be flawed and not feel bad about
it.

Don't look for that space in other people.
Not because you can't find it,
but how long you'll get to own it depends
on how long they stay in your life.

Yours truly,
*Myself*

Dear Self,

Be cautious about what you say to
and about yourself, or how you say it.
The subtle harmful jokes and compliments
you reject because you feel unworthy.

Talk to yourself the way you would to someone you love.

Yours truly,
*Myself*

Dear Self,

I hope so well for you.

I hope that;
you give your all to your craft,
nothing makes you doubt your best,
you don't compare yourself to others,
you're being patient with what you start.

I hope that;
you're healing every day,
you've surrounded yourself with love, enough
to keep your heart warm, you anticipate more
than just disappointment for the future.

I hope that;
every day teaches you something valuable,
doors of opportunity are opened for you,
you reach your goals.

Oh, but most of all,
Dear Self, I hope you're happy and content wherever you
are.

Yours truly,
*Myself*

Dear Self,

You're not your circumstances.
You're not your weaknesses.
You're not your failures.
You're not your emotions.
You're not your qualifications.
You're not your thoughts.
Anything that isn't a constant doesn't define you.
You're more than that.

What you can or cannot do, isn't all there is to who you are.

Yours truly,
*Myself*

Dear Self,

In pursuit of your dreams,
don't forget that it will not be easy.
Some days it won't make sense at all to pursue them.
But it'll be easier on others, and that'll be the best feeling ever.
Despite the kind of day you're having,
your dreams are valid and attainable.

Never allow the voices in your head to make you give up,
quiet them down with compassion, affirmations and love,
because not every day is going to be a bad day.

Learn to surf your way through the unpleasant days,
because all you've ever dreamed of, you deserve.

Yours truly,
*Myself*

Dear Self,

There's so much that could stand in your way,
delay your progress,
hinder you from achieving certain things,
stop you from trying something out,
but ensure that you're not the one standing in your way.

Pay attention to how you speak to yourself,
cheer yourself on,
do not cease developing yourself,
go for everything you want to go for,
and do what you would've done before
you convinced yourself that you can't.

Yours truly,
*Myself*

Dear Self,

Please remember that you're able to thrive
in every situation, life throws at you,
you get through every challenge, one way or another,
and you're never stuck.

Not all plans get fulfilled
but don't be discouraged.
It will work out for the best
as long as you keep going.

Yours truly,
*Myself*

Dear Self,

The last thing you should ever find
yourself aiming for is being average.
An excellent God created you.
Look in the mirror and see that brilliance.

Don't settle for a version of yourself that is
lower than who you were made to be.
With each day that goes by,
I hope you learn how to embrace who you are.

Yours truly,
*Myself*

Dear Self,

Growing in self-awareness is the most significant
gift you can ever give to yourself.
Knowing who you are
and understanding your patterns.
Despite the discomfort, this might come with,
that is the best thing you can ever do for yourself.

Get to a point in your self-awareness journey where
nothing you do, say, or feel comes off as a surprise.

Yours truly,
*Myself*

Dear Self,

Maybe loving yourself more also means that you stop
certain things.
Stop expecting from other people what you can do for
yourself,
stop expecting people to understand you,
stop feeling the need to over-explain yourself,
stop regarding other people more than you actually
consider yourself.

Cautiously let people in,
but don't let their opinions or beliefs quiet down your
voice,
because it matters just as much, or maybe even more.

Yours truly,
*Myself*

Dear Self,

You deserve love.
The kind of love that understands,
and knows when to put others first.
Love that is pure, patient, and unconditional.

Yours truly,
*Myself*

Dear Self,

Don't ever let how people choose to treat you
influence how you see yourself.
You're valuable and deserving.
Don't be one of the people who
constantly fail to see that.

Yours truly,
*Myself*

Dear Self,

I choose you with all your flaws, failures, wins,
strengths and weaknesses.
Over and over again, I choose you.

Yours truly,
*Myself*

Dear Self,

In these years of your life
I hope you surround yourself with love,
in friendships, family, romantic relationships,
in God and, most importantly, within yourself.
I pray that you experience it in its purest form,
and that it makes life a little bearable for you.

Yours truly,
*Myself*

Dear Self,

No matter how hard it gets,
I want you to thrive,
to be resilient,
to fight until you win.
And when you don't win?
I want you to still look in the
mirror and still see gold.

Yours truly,
*Myself*

Dear Self,

You've always been enough. Always.

Yours truly,
*Myself*

Dear Self,

This is a reminder
that each time you make a decision,
it is the best decision you could make at that moment.
Whether or not it turns out to be the right one,
you did what you thought was best.

Yours truly,
*Myself*

# Collection III

*Affirmations*

(14)

Everything falls into place, eventually.

I'll do my best in everything,
if it doesn't turn out as I expect,
I will not be hard on myself.

Things don't always go according to plan,
and that's okay.

I am doing the best I can.

This is where I'm supposed to be, and that's on God.

I will not pay attention to things that negatively shift my energy.

My hard work will yield results.

I am not my anxiety, sadness or failures.

Someday, I will heal from everything that has hurt me.
But until then, I will be kind to myself.

I have inside of me everything I need to live a bountiful life.

I deserve love,
in its purest and most certain form.

I've robbed myself of the chance to
make mistakes and learn from them.
Different circumstances remind me that
I'm imperfect, and it's completely okay.
In this new journey, I choose to embrace myself still.

I'm taking things one step at a time.
I will not expect myself to get it right all the way through,
I will do my best when I can.
And I'll be proud of the progress I make,
Regardless of how big or small it is.

I'm going to take it easy.
We're all doing this life
thing for the first time.

# Final Thoughts

Self-love is a lifetime journey,
and you are worth being dedicated a lifetime for.
I hope that you continue trying to learn your love language.
Here's to exploring, learning, unlearning, living, and loving yourself more.

One last thing before you go. If you enjoyed reading this book or found it helpful in any way, please give it a review on Amazon (https://amzn.to/3STLhX1). It will mean a lot that you took your precious time to help me reach someone else.

# About the Author

Duduzile Noeleen Ngwenya is a writer and digital entrepreneur from Pretoria, South Africa. She founded Ayana Magazine, a digital women magazine, in 2017. She discovered her passion for self-development as she soared through her early twenties. She has made it her life's mission to inspire others to grow in self-love and acceptance, that way she is also challenged to grow. Full bio on:

https://www.amazon.com/author/duduzilengwenya